MADE NEW

HOW GOD CHANGES EVERYTHING

PRESENTED TO

Amarthya B.

BY

Jia Glendy

DATE

July 13, 2024

Baptism on June 30, 2024.

Lifeway Press®
Brentwood, Tennessee

ISBN 978-1-0877-8477-9
Item 005842349
Dewey Decimal Classification Number: 242
Subject Heading: DEVOTIONAL LITERATURE / BIBLE STUDY AND TEACHING / GOD

Printed in the United States of America.

Student Ministry Publishing
Lifeway Resources
200 Powell Place, Suite 100
Brentwood, Tennessee 37027

We believe that the Bible has God for its author; salvation for its end; truth, without any mixture of error, for its matter; and that all Scripture is totally true and trustworthy. To review Lifeway's doctrinal guideline, please visit www.lifeway.com/doctrinalguideline.

publishing team

Director, Student Ministry
Ben Trueblood

Manager, Student Publishing
Karen Daniel

Writer
Leslie Hudson

Content Editor
Kyle Wiltshire

Production Editor
April-Lyn Caouette

Graphic Designers
Shiloh Stufflebeam
Grace Morgan

TABLE OF
CONTENTS

INTRO

New. Sit still for a minute and think about the meaning of that word. Something that's new isn't just something old that looks nice. It's not something that's been recycled or reused or refurbished. It's something that's never been used before. Untouched. Pristine.

Everyone loves new things. Like new clothes: they smell different, look different, and feel different. It's always cool when we get to live, work, or worship in a new building. Often, we're drawn to new video games, new music, and new shows. We look forward to a new season, a new day, or a new school year. Why are we all drawn to new things? Sometimes it's because we need a new start.

What if you could get that new start? What if you could be made new? What if your mind, heart, and life could be made new? What if you could get a new attitude, a new purpose, and a new focus? Believe it or not, you can. The Bible doesn't just say that it's possible—Scripture promises that we can all be made new.

You're probably thinking, "That sounds good and all, but 'new' isn't all it's cracked up to be." New shoes look shabby pretty fast. New buildings lose that fresh-paint smell. New games and new opportunities lose their luster as we get comfortable with them. This is all true.

But a new you? That may seem crazy, but it's absolutely real. Jesus—and only Jesus—can make you new. The One who made everything can make you new, inside and out, and as you go through this book over the next thirty days, you'll see how.

GETTING STARTED

This devotional contains thirty days of content, broken down into sections. Each day is divided into three elements—**discover**, **delight**, and **display**—to help you grow in your faith and guide your time in God's Word.

DISCOVER

This section helps you examine the passage in light of who God is and determine what it says about your identity in relationship to Him. Included here is the daily Scripture reading and key verses, along with illustrations and commentary to guide you as you learn more about God's Word.

DELIGHT

In this section, you'll be challenged by questions and activities that help you see how God is alive and active in every detail of His Word and in your life.

DISPLAY

Here's where you take action. This section calls you to apply what you've learned through each day.

Each day also includes a prayer activity at the conclusion of the devotion.

Throughout the devotional, you'll also find extra items to help you connect with the topic personally, such as Scripture memory verses and interactive articles.

A NEW CREATION

Jesus has all authority in heaven and on earth. He created, sustains, and rules everything in the universe, down to the tiniest particle. With that power, He makes us new; not just better or improved versions of ourselves, but completely new in Him. Over these next ten days, we'll learn how.

THE GREAT EXCHANGE

READ 2 CORINTHIANS 5:16-21.

*Therefore, if anyone is in Christ, he is a new creation; the old
has passed away, and see, the new has come!*
— 2 Corinthians 5:17

DISCOVER

When you read today's passage, how did it sound in your head? Was it in
a monotone? Please read it again, aloud if possible, and this time, read
it as though you had the world's biggest secret and you were dying to
share it.

That's probably how Paul meant it as he wrote. For good reason: this is
amazing news! When we are saved through faith in Jesus, we come to
see Him with spiritual eyes of faith, not through earthly eyes. Anyone
who is in Christ, who has chosen to entrust his or her life now and
eternally to Him as Savior and Lord, is a new creation. The old person, the
pre-Jesus self, is gone.

This passage tells us that God reconciled us to Himself through Jesus.
One meaning of the word "reconciliation" relates to finances—it means
to exchange or to make a debt correct. We come to God with nothing
on our own, but God basically says, "You're with Jesus? You don't owe
anything!" He forgives us of our sins and entrusts us with the lifelong task
of spreading the message of this reconciliation to others.

This is what Christians are called to do: we speak God's truth. Paul calls us
Christ's ambassadors (v. 20), meaning we go on His behalf to our friends,
family, acquaintances, and beyond. While this is our mission, the death
and resurrection of Jesus is how we are made new. Anyone can receive
God's reconciliation if she or he is in Jesus through saving faith. Jesus
became the payment for our sins; that's a great exchange!

Consider verse 16 carefully. What changes about our perspective when we come to saving faith in Jesus?

How do you see Jesus and others differently today than you used to?

How do you know you are a new creation? What have you or others observed about you that proves it?

DISPLAY

Consider writing the word "new" on a card where you'll see it many times over the thirty days you'll be studying this theme. Each time you look at it, let your mind consider the truths from Scripture that tell you that you are a new creation. Remind yourself: "The old me is gone; the new me is here!" Challenge yourself to consider each day's truth and apply it to your life. For example, the "old you" may have lost your cool quickly; the "new you" chooses to have patience, grace, and forgiveness.

As you pray today, read back through 2 Corinthians 5:16-21, changing the word "we" to "I" each time you see it. Prayerfully consider, "Are these promised truths of a new creation true about my life?" Invite the Holy Spirit to show you how you have changed, grown, and matured in your faith.

BIG LETTERS

READ GALATIANS 6:11-18.

For both circumcision and uncircumcision mean
nothing; what matters instead is a new creation.
— Galatians 6:15

DISCOVER

Paul wrote with passion and expression; you see that here in verse 11 as he writes about the large letters he used to stress the importance of his subject. Imagine getting Paul's letters with some of the words written in all caps, double sized!

Paul's Christian friends in Galatia were struggling. There were people coming into their churches who were born and raised as Jews, and these people were telling Christians that to follow Jesus, they also had to follow the Jewish law. The thinking went like this: Jesus was a Jew, and since God had brought Jesus out of the lineage of Abraham, Jewish laws must be fulfilled in order to follow Jesus.

Paul knew this wasn't true; following the law had nothing to do with salvation! These Jewish Christians simply wanted a reason to boast—to brag about themselves. It would be like telling your friends you were a great Christian because you wear your cross necklace every day. It might seem nice on the surface, but it has nothing at all to do with faith.

With big letters, Paul cut to the chase: nothing outward is worth boasting about. The cross of Jesus is the only reason to brag, and being made new through Jesus is the only thing that matters. Paul had the scars to prove he was completely devoted to Jesus (v. 17) but he didn't show them off. He was a new creation, and he was confident in his identity in Christ.

Have you been guilty of doing something lately that is a passive form of bragging about your faith? What would Paul say about that?

What does it mean to boast about the cross of Jesus?

Spend a few minutes today journaling about what Christ has done for you. When did He save you? How did you hear His truth? Who helped you understand the gospel? How are you living out your faith today? How are you sharing Jesus with others? By answering these questions, you are boasting in the cross and focusing on His work in your life rather than your own work. As you write, consider an opportunity in which you might have the chance to speak these words aloud to someone this week. Boasting in Jesus strengthens our faith, encourages other believers, and spreads the message of salvation.

Boasting in Jesus takes courage and faith. As you pray today, confess the areas in which you are timid, bashful, afraid, or nervous at the thought of sharing the message of Jesus. Ask the Holy Spirit to give you the right words at the right time, and ask Jesus to strengthen your faith to believe Him as you carry His message out into the world.

HEAVENLY FOCUS

READ COLOSSIANS 3:1-4.

For you died, and your life is hidden with Christ in God.
— Colossians 3:3

DISCOVER

Paul opens today's passage with the statement, "So if you have been raised with Christ." This idea of "being raised with Christ" has many different names, such as getting saved, becoming a Christian, or following Jesus. "Being raised with Christ" describes people who have turned to Jesus alone for life, eternity, and salvation.

If this is you, Paul has further instructions for you. First, "seek the things above, where Christ is" (v. 1). That might seem like a strange instruction. How can we seek the things in heaven? We can't even see it! Precisely. We turn our utmost attention to the things that can't be seen: God's perfect plan, the characteristics of Jesus, His will for our lives, and how to best make His glory known.

If your focus is on "earthly things" (v. 2), it will be on the visible: clothing, money, image, and more. But these earthly things aren't of any importance to someone who has died to self and has chosen to live for Jesus (see Luke 9:23). Instead, our lives are wrapped up in Jesus. He is our focus and our goal. We believe that He will one day be visible to every eye, even though for now we choose to focus on the One we cannot see. And when He returns, we will join Him because we glorified Him on earth. This heavenly focus is the goal of one who has been made a new creation, one who has been made new in Jesus.

Carefully consider the word "seek" in verse 1. What does it mean to "seek the things above"?

What does it mean to be "hidden in Christ with God" (v. 3)?

DISPLAY

As new creations, we must consider our lives wrapped up in Jesus. This means we change our focus to His desires as we set our minds on things above. In your Bible study journal, begin a list entitled "Seeking Things Above." As you read through the Bible, hear sermons, or ponder the truths of the Bible, jot down the things your mind considers that are "things above, not . . . earthly things" (v. 2). For today's passage, you might write, "Christ is seated at the right hand of God." That's certainly a heavenly thought! Consider how that reality shapes your faith today.

Before you pray today, spend two minutes getting a picture of heaven in your mind. (If you have no idea what heaven is like, read Revelation 4.) Ask God to help you believe the truth of heaven and His place on the throne. Sing a brief song of worship before you begin your prayer.

DAY 4

NEW YOU

READ COLOSSIANS 3:5-11.

*In Christ there is not Greek and Jew, circumcision and uncircumcision,
barbarian, Scythian, slave and free; but Christ is all and in all.*
— Colossians 3:11

DISCOVER

Yesterday, we considered Paul's instruction to set our minds on things
above—heavenly things, which do not overlap with the things of
the world. Today's Scripture, which immediately follows the verses
from yesterday, moves from having our minds on heavenly things to
considering how that impacts our lives.

Paul gives us two lists. The first list contains things that we must put to
death: sexual immorality, impurity, lust, evil desire, and greed. Much of
our world is marked by these choices, but Christians must choose to focus
on God rather than these selfish mindsets. Paul then commands us to put
away anger, wrath, malice, slander, and filthy language. The instruction
to "put away" something brings to mind a teacher instructing you to put
away your phones: they are a distraction that have a negative impact on
your proper focus.

The next instruction deals with lying: don't do it. Lying has no place in the
new creation that we become through saving faith in Jesus. Lying is what
our old self did; the new self must reject all lying.

Don't miss the exciting truth about our new identity in verse 10. We are
being renewed in knowledge according to the image of God! Every time
we learn something new from the Bible, we are being made even more
new! The more we understand Jesus, the more we become like Him.

Christ takes away every division and allows us all to have one identity: His!
So kill those old ways and live like the new you.

Paul lists several attitudes, thoughts, and actions to avoid. Which of these do you find hardest to "put away"?

How common are these things in the world among your friends, your family, and people at school? How might living opposite those things allow you to be a witness for Jesus?

DISPLAY

Imagine putting something to death—it's a gruesome image, right? But Paul doesn't want us to miss the passion in his words: we must kill sin if we're truly saved. We don't let it stick around and we don't pretend it isn't there. We kill it. As you see sin of any kind creep into your mind, words, or actions, don't mess around. Stop, confess your sin, and ask Jesus how to kill that sin. It might involve changing your relationships, your habits, or your mindset. But He will give you the insight and courage to do it.

As you pray today, slowly read back through Colossians 3:5-11. Let your eyes rest on each of the lists of sins that Paul tells us we must kill or put away. For each item, ask the Holy Spirit to reveal where you struggle in that sin, and ask Him for His help.

DAY 5

DRESSED IN THE NEW

READ COLOSSIANS 3:12-14.

Above all, put on love, which is the perfect bond of unity.
— Colossians 3:14

DISCOVER

If you haven't realized, these last few days have been back-to-back passages from Colossians 3. (And tomorrow's will be too!) Through all these words, Paul is building upon the truths that we're raised with Christ (vv. 1-4) and we put sin to death (vv. 5-11). Today's passage starts with "therefore," which is Paul's way of saying, "Because of all that Christ has done for you, here's how you live."

First, we know and believe that we are chosen, holy, and loved by God. Pause right there and focus on those three identities: chosen, holy, loved. Because of who we are in Christ, we choose to take on His characteristics: compassion, kindness, humility, gentleness, and patience. We bear with one another, and we forgive one another freely.

You might argue, "But nobody lives like that." Exactly! Nobody—except people who have been made new by Jesus. If you've ever met someone who is truly compassionate, kind, humble, gentle, patient, and forgiving, you know what an impact one life can make on the world.

All of our demonstrations of Christ in us can be summed up in one word: love. Because of the love God has for us, He sent Jesus (see John 3:16). And because we love God, we show His love to others. Above all, we put on love, which binds us together as believers. "Above all" is a great phrase: despite our fears or our doubts, regardless of our day or our attitude, we choose to love. That is what a new creation does.

Look carefully at verses 12 and 14. What two-word phrase do both of these verses instruct you to do? How do we do this?

What image comes to mind when you consider this instruction found in verses 12 and 14? How easy is it to follow?

DISPLAY

Tomorrow, as you put on your clothes for the day, mentally picture yourself also putting on compassion, kindness, humility, gentleness, and patience. Carefully consider what that looks like when a teacher gives you a pop quiz, a friend has a snarky attitude, or you and your parents don't see eye to eye. If you struggle to desire these characteristics in yourself, consider the love Jesus showed you on the cross and thank Him for His sacrifice. As you choose to love above all else, choose also to forgive often. It won't be easy, but Jesus will help you as you pour out your life for Him.

Notice that Paul's words in today's passage aren't to one person, but to a group: the Christians in Colossae. Hear these instructions not just for yourself but for your youth group, your Christian friends, and your church. Pray today that God will give you all a desire for love and unity for one another.

DAY 6

IN EVERYTHING? REALLY?

READ COLOSSIANS 3:15-17.

And whatever you do, in word or in deed, do everything in the name of the Lord Jesus, giving thanks to God the Father through him.
— Colossians 3:17

DISCOVER

Paul opens our Scripture today with a word that instructs us to look back, so if you don't remember what you've been reading in Colossians 3, go back and review it!

Paul is in the middle of teaching us what it means to walk in faith as a lifestyle. In addition to the instructions he gave in verses 12-14, he adds a few more. First, we "let the peace of Christ...rule [our] hearts" (v. 15). In Christ, we have peace with God and peace for eternity. From that, we find that we can also have peace with others, with our situations, and with ourselves. Because of that peace, we choose to "be thankful" (v. 15), acknowledging God for His good gifts through Jesus. As we study the Bible, letting it "dwell richly" in us (v. 16), we speak those words to others, teaching and encouraging and showing them grace.

Next, Paul gives a general overview of living in the peace of Christ. Do everything—*everything?* Yes, everything—in the name of Jesus. As ambassadors for Christ (remember from Day 1, 2 Cor. 5:20), we represent Him as we go throughout our day. That's what "in the name of the Lord Jesus" means—we're sent by Him and we show others who He is. We don't power through this divine assignment on our own; we thank God that we get to walk in faith! Thankfulness (v. 15) comes forth from our lips and we verbally give thanks (v. 17) to Him.

MADE NEW

Would you say your life is marked by peace? What does verse 15 reveal about how to get there?

In order to "let the word of Christ dwell richly among you" (v. 16), what must you be doing on a daily basis? Do you?

Throughout all of the letters of Paul that we have in the Bible, Paul gives many instructions on how to live the Christian life. But today's key verse is a great summary of all of them: do everything in the name of the Lord Jesus, giving thanks to God. It seems so simple, but it's not easy! Consider one or two difficult circumstances you'll handle today. Then ask yourself: *How would this reveal Jesus to people in my life? How can I thank God for this situation?* As you go through the day, ask the Lord to make your words and deeds an accurate response as His representative.

As you pray today, focus on the words "peace" and "thankful." Notice that your peace comes from Christ—not from your situation, your friends, or your own mindset. Ask Jesus to show you how to let the peace of Christ rule your heart. Thank Him for giving you that peace, and keep thanking Him silently throughout the day. Thank Him for making you a new creation.

THEREFORE, IF
ANYONE IS IN
CHRIST, HE IS A

NEW

CREATION; THE
OLD HAS PASSED
AWAY, AND SEE,
THE NEW HAS COME!

2 CORINTHIANS 5:17

WHAT'S YOUR HEART MADE OF?

READ EZEKIEL 36:16-38.

" 'I will give you a new heart and put a new spirit within you; I will remove your heart of stone and give you a heart of flesh.' "
— Ezekiel 36:26

DISCOVER

Ezekiel wrote his prophecies down hundreds of years before Jesus was born. God's chosen people—the Israelites—had lived idolatrous, sinful lives, and Ezekiel revealed God's displeasure. But sprinkled throughout the judgment, Ezekiel also described God's blessings and favor. The Israelites hadn't deserved it, but God wanted the nations to know who He was (v. 23) through His actions on behalf of the Israelites.

God's greatest blessing to the Israelites wouldn't be rebuilt cities or replanted fields: it would be a new heart and new spirit. These internal changes would not only be detectable to God's people but to everyone who came into contact with them.

God does the same for us: He takes our hard, stony (unrepentant, stubborn, selfish, idolatrous) hearts and gives us soft ones that are gentle, teachable, and willing to change. He also takes our spirits—our disposition, our courage, our temper, our anger, and everything else about us—and gives us a new one: His Holy Spirit (v. 27), which dwells in and among us.

God's people had wandered far from Him, but He also knew that they would return. He would fulfill this promise of a new heart and new spirit. As we turn back to Him, He does the same for us.

When did your heart reflect a "heart of stone" (v. 26)? How did your hard heart affect your relationships and your faith?

According to verse 27, what happens when we have God's Spirit within us? How has His Spirit changed you?

God's plan for us is the same plan He had for the Israelites: to let everyone on earth know that He is the Lord (v. 23). He offers us the chance to be clean and free from sin and idolatry. But we must accept Him as our Lord before He works in us. "Lord" is another word for "master." Is Jesus the Master of your life? Do you obey, submit, and listen carefully? Do you follow His instructions to love, forgive, help, serve, and give hope? These are the marks of one who has given Him lordship over his or her life.

As you pray today, ask the Lord to show you how your heart is different today than it was before you came to saving faith in Jesus. As you've grown physically, have you grown spiritually as well? Or is your heart unchanged? Offer your confession to God and ask Him to continue to give you the new heart and new spirit you desperately need.

HEART SCRUBBED CLEAN

READ PSALM 51.

God, create a clean heart for me and renew a steadfast spirit within me.
— Psalm 51:10

DISCOVER

If your Bible gives a short description for each of the psalms, don't miss this one. It probably says something like, "A psalm of David, when the prophet Nathan came to him after he had gone to Bathsheba." If you don't know the story, you can read it in 2 Samuel 11, but to summarize, David had committed sexual sin with Bathsheba, which led to him lying and murdering her husband, Uriah, one of David's finest soldiers.

David had been called a man after God's own heart (see 1 Sam. 13:14). He had demonstrated his devotion to listening, obeying, and seeking to glorify God. But in the blink of an eye, David had egregiously sinned and then started making one bad decision after another.

This psalm is the song David composed after he was confronted by the prophet Nathan (see 2 Sam. 12:1-15). His opening words are telling: he asks for God's grace, love, compassion, and forgiveness because he had been rebellious. David didn't try to hide his sin; he was guilty and only God's forgiveness could cleanse him from it. He had hurt many people along the way, but he realized that he had ultimately sinned not against them but against God. We do the same thing when we disregard His commands and go our own way.

But even when we stumble, God offers us forgiveness, a clean heart, and a renewed spirit. We can't do it ourselves and we can't do anything to deserve it. But God loves us enough that, even when we've sinned, He will give us a new heart.

Read through this entire psalm, slowly and carefully. Which phrase stands out to you? Why?

In your Bible, underline each of the descriptions of God in Psalm 51. Summarize those words into one sentence.

In considering this entire story, we can see that David made two big decisions. First, he chose to sin. Like David, we will fall into temptation and be guilty of sin. But second, David chose to confess his sin and seek God's mercy and forgiveness. The Lord is God of every mercy, and He extends this mercy to everyone who comes humbly seeking forgiveness. Psalm 51 is a great prayer for when you find yourself in sin; pray it in those times. It will remind you of who God is and how He responds to your repentant heart.

As you enter your time of prayer, briefly glance back through Psalm 51. Some verses focus on sin and confession; others look squarely at the character of God. Choose one or two verses and make them your prayer for the day. Thank God for this recorded prayer of David that is your prayer, as well.

DAY 9

JUST IMAGINE

READ ISAIAH 65:17-25.

"For I will create new heavens and a new earth; the past events will not be remembered or come to mind."
— Isaiah 65:17

DISCOVER

Did you play "make-believe" when you were a kid? Maybe you pretended you were royalty, or a pirate, or a wilderness explorer. Maybe you pretended with your dolls, your stuffed animals, or even your friends.

Today's passage sounds a little bit like make-believe; it describes a perfect place and a perfect world. Of course, that doesn't exist . . . right? Right now, you are correct. This current world can never be perfect in every way. For that reason, God is going to start over with a new heaven and a new earth.

Perfection is coming. There will be no crying (v. 19), no childhood death (v. 20), no one forced to evacuate (v. 21), no unfair taking of property (v. 22), and no evil (v. 25). God's perfect plan for His people will cause us all to rejoice, and we will all find delight in it. We'll live forever, in the presence of God, rejoicing and witnessing perfection.

How is this possible? The new heavens and new earth won't have any sin or any of the things that come from it, like sickness, hurt, harm, or death. Not only will there not be sin, but God won't even remember our sin from the past: "The past events will not be remembered or come to mind" (v. 17). You won't remember them, I won't remember them, and God won't remember them. Perfection isn't here yet, but we can celebrate that God has promised it. One day, we'll join Him and be made new there!

DELIGHT

The phrase "I will" appears five times in today's passage. Find each of these five times in your Bible and underline them. What comfort do you take from these "I will" statements?

According to what you underlined, what will God do in the new heavens and earth? How should we respond to that news?

In verse 17, God promises new heavens and a new earth. In verse 18, we are commanded: "Then be glad and rejoice forever in what I am creating." The Bible is full of God's promises and how He is faithful to follow through every single time. This prophecy is one of those promises! Though this reality is not here yet, we can be glad and rejoice every day because we believe that it will be. So as you go through your day today, keep the words "be glad and rejoice forever" in the back of your mind; put a smile on your face and let these words be the song of your heart!

Whom do you need to pray for today? As you consider your list, lift up people who are sick, hurting, struggling, and mourning; those are terrible things. But then read Isaiah 65:17-25 aloud again, and thank God for His promised new heavens and earth, where those things will cease to be.

DAY 10

WE WAIT!

READ 2 PETER 3:1-13.

*But based on his promise, we wait for new heavens and
a new earth, where righteousness dwells.*
— 2 Peter 3:13

DISCOVER

Yesterday, in Isaiah 65, you considered God's promise of a new heaven
and a new earth, untainted by sin and all its effects. Perhaps since
you read that passage yesterday you thought, "Yeah, right. That was
thousands of years ago! This is taking forever!"

Well, Peter anticipated that. You remember Peter, right? He was one
of Jesus's closest disciples and a leader of the early church. He wrote
the words you read today, and he anticipated that people would
doubt God's promises for the future. He predicted that people would
scoff (v. 3)—that they would laugh in disbelief. But Peter reminds us: God
created all the worlds and heavens long ago. He oversaw all that has ever
happened on earth, and He will one day judge it and start the new one.

God isn't slow—He's patient. He's full of mercy and compassion before
beginning His new kingdom. It will happen quickly, and it's going to be
crazy. But we who know Jesus have nothing to fear; in fact, we anticipate
these prophecies with excitement! Righteousness and holiness will dwell
with us in this new heavens and earth. It's going to be amazing!

So as we wait, what do we do? We live like new creations who believe it's
coming! We live in "holy conduct and godliness" (v. 11) as a testament to
our faith in God's promise and our anticipation of that new place.

According to verses 3-4, what are some things scoffers say? What are they ignoring (v. 5)?

What does verse 8 mean? How does this passage give you hope as you wait on God's promises?

DISPLAY

As believers, we are called to see God's promises as truth. Your unsaved friends and family members probably don't want to think about end times, and most people prefer not even to consider their own death. As Christians walk with rejoicing toward an uncertain future, we point to the faithfulness of God. Consider how your faith is revealed in your conversations about sickness, death, and the unsure state of the world. Don't ignore your fears of these topics, but take them to the Lord in prayer and discuss them with a parent, mentor, pastor, or Bible teacher you trust.

As you get ready to pray, read through verses 10-13 again, slowly and aloud if possible. Then close your eyes and consider for just a moment what that event will do to everything in the world. Perhaps you hear the noise, see the flames, and picture the reaction of most people. Ask God to give you faith to believe but also to tell unbelievers the truth of these words.

A NEW MIND

How would you describe your mind? Free-flowing? Unfocused? Determined? Tightly closed? The mind is the center of thought, barely understood by even the most brilliant scientists. And yet Jesus gives us a new mind as He transforms us to be like Him. Have you let Him change your mind yet? Now is the perfect time.

INSIDE OUT

READ ROMANS 12:1-2.

Do not be conformed to this age, but be transformed by
the renewing of your mind, so that you may discern what is
the good, pleasing, and perfect will of God.
— Romans 12:2

DISCOVER

In Romans 11, Paul wrote some strong words for Christian believers. After the Jews—even though they were God's chosen people—rejected Him, God brought the Gentiles—non-Jews—into His household. Paul warned the Gentiles that being chosen by God doesn't guarantee a faithful walk; just like the Jews, Christians can sometimes choose to disregard God as well.

So we come to the opening words of Romans 12: because of His mercy, we should live sacrificial lives, holy and pleasing to God. We might think of sacrifice as choosing a more difficult route than others, but the imagery was different for these first-century Christians. To them, sacrifice meant the death of an animal to cover sin. For Old Testament believers, worship meant offering a sacrifice to God. For New Testament believers, the sacrifice is our very selves. But we don't lose our lives; instead we live our lives for Him, holy and pleasing. We accomplish this not by looking like everyone else in our culture but by allowing God to renew our minds, transforming us and changing us to think like He does.

The verbs "be conformed" and "be transformed" in verse 2 are passive verbs—being conformed and transformed isn't something we do but something that happens to us. In order to not be conformed to society, we must choose to let God change us from the mind outward. When we do, we clearly see the "good, pleasing, and perfect will of God" (v. 2).

According to verse 1, what is the primary reason we choose to live sacrificial lives and let God transform us?

When we let God transform our minds, what happens to our lives?

DISPLAY

When Jesus died once and for all for our sin, the system of blood sacrifice was finished. Instead, we live a holy life because of the merciful and perfect sacrifice of Jesus. Part of that sacrificial life means giving God the right to transform our ways of thinking and seeing. God-renewed minds don't think like the rest of the world; they think in terms of the truth of God's kingdom. Carefully consider your own thought life: Do you really hold God's standards to be ultimate truth? Do those standards guide your words, actions, and attitudes? As you reflect on your answers to these questions, pray and ask God to renew your mind today.

As you prepare to pray, zoom in on the words "in view of the mercies of God" in verse 1. When was the last time you focused on the mercies of God—His unearned grace, His unlimited love, and His unbelievable sacrifice? Focus on His mercies, and then voice your prayers of thanksgiving to Him.

DAY 12

ACCURATE ASSESSMENT

READ ROMANS 12:3-8.

For by the grace given to me, I tell everyone among you not to think of himself more highly than he should think. Instead, think sensibly, as God has distributed a measure of faith to each one.
— Romans 12:3

DISCOVER

Most of us struggle to see ourselves accurately. You've seen it online or on television: a person claims to be amazing at dancing, singing, or skateboarding . . . but then he performs and you realize that he overestimated his abilities. On the other hand, many of us think too lowly about ourselves. We are too critical of our outward appearances, our personalities, and our talents. Neither our self-hatred nor our self-pride is usually accurate. Neither is biblical, either.

To have a renewed mind, we must not think too highly of ourselves or too lowly. We need to see ourselves accurately. In today's verses, Paul invites us to consider the facts: God has given everyone faith (v. 3) and we are all parts of one body (v. 4) where everyone functions differently but together (vv. 4-8).

In light of that, we should "think sensibly," remembering that everything is given to us by the grace of God, and everything we do is for His glory, not our own. When we know and believe this truth, we are choosing to think about ourselves accurately (v. 3). That's an amazing testimony! God puts us into a body of believers where we are humble because of our role in God's kingdom and where we work with others in unity.

DELIGHT

Re-read verse 4 and look at the sketch of a body below. Spiritually speaking, who reminds you of a brain, a heart, or a hand? Write their names in the appropriate spot next to the diagram.

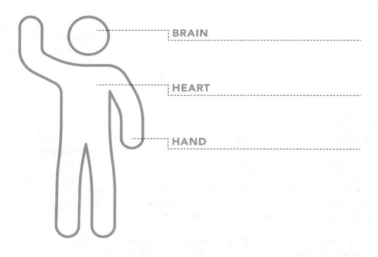

BRAIN

HEART

HAND

How many times do you see the word "grace" in this passage? What does that indicate to you?

DISPLAY

God's grace enabled Paul to see himself and other believers in a sensible way: every person is important, valuable, and called to work together with one another, but no one person stands out as better than others. This is what a healthy, God-honoring body of believers looks like. How are you inspiring unity and sensible thinking in your family, youth group, or church? Take some time to thank God for His grace and the spiritual gifts He has given you. Find your place in your body of faith and live boldly for God's glory in the congregation

As you pray today, read verse 3 aloud slowly. Ask God to reveal the areas in your life where you don't see yourself accurately and where you don't think sensibly. If you struggle here, go back to verses 1-2, remembering that your thinking is being transformed by the renewing of your mind. Wait patiently for Him to make you new in your thinking!

NEW MIND, NEW LIFE

READ ROMANS 12:9-14.

Bless those who persecute you; bless and do not curse.
— Romans 12:14

DISCOVER

There is an epidemic in our world today: snarkiness. You know what snarkiness is, right? It's when someone replies with a biting, mean-spirited, or sarcastic remark. It's hard to have a conversation today without a snarky comment weaseling its way in.

Perhaps you've noticed something about Jesus: He didn't conform to the world around Him. As His disciples, we're not supposed to, either. In fact, Romans 12:2 instructs us to "not be conformed to this age, but be transformed by the renewing of your mind." A transformed—new—mind is great, and it is revealed in a transformed life.

So what might a transformed life look like? Well, today's passage points to a lack of snarkiness: loving what is good, loving one another, honoring each other, and avoiding hypocrisy. On top of that, we choose to be passionate for God (v. 11), revealing our faith as we live as hopeful, patient, prayerful people. These instructions are clearly easy to understand but difficult to live out! And Paul continues: share with people in need, be hospitable, and bless those who persecute you.

You might think that last one is a joke. It sounds impossible! But it's actually an outpouring of a life changed by the love and mercy of Christ. Followers of Jesus are so changed by His Spirit that they can choose to get rid of snarkiness, indifference, and selfishness. As we live in Christ, we should never be content to blend in. We should stand out as we live out our faith!

Almost every sentence in these verses begins with an instructive verb; underline them in your Bible. Which one of these is the easiest for you? Which one is the hardest?

Do you know someone who often carries out these instructions? Who is it? How does that person's faith encourage yours?

DISPLAY

Today's Scripture contains a list of several short instructions. Don't get overwhelmed! As you read through the list you might think, "I'm not doing any of those things!" But that's why you are allowing Jesus to transform your mind: He will enable you to obey them! Today, write all of these instructions on a piece of paper and choose one to work on. Then tomorrow, choose another. You'll never obey them all perfectly, but as you follow hard after Jesus, you'll find that He is faithful to strengthen and guide you.

We're hesitant to bless others when we don't feel blessed ourselves. Before you pray today, write ten blessings in your life right now, and thank God aloud for each of those. Then ask Him to show you how you can be a blessing today. Walk through your day with eyes of faith, looking for an opportunity to live obediently.

INTENTIONAL COMPASSION

READ ROMANS 12:15-21.

If possible, as far as it depends on you, live at peace with everyone.
— Romans 12:18

DISCOVER

Yesterday, our Scripture reading included several instructions for how to live as followers of Christ who are learning to let Him transform our minds. In today's passage, the list continues. Pastors can easily preach on each of these instructions for an hour, so don't rush through the list! These are valuable, precious instructions for new minds and genuine lives of faith.

Yesterday's verses instructed us to love without hypocrisy, even toward our enemies. In today's verses, the stress is on compassion: we rejoice with those who are happy and weep with those who are weeping (v. 15). Is that awkward sometimes? Sure! But when we enter into celebrating and mourning with others, we show them genuine love and compassion.

The remainder of this passage points to getting along with others. There is nothing here that gets us off the hook; "Live in harmony with one another" (v. 16) is pretty straightforward. We choose peace, we choose love, and we choose to be people who aren't proud (v. 16). We're humble, thoughtful, and we don't give ourselves credit for being too wise. We should even go so far as to not retaliate when people treat us cruelly.

We can't change people, and we can't force them to be kind. But the key verse reminds us: "As far as it depends on you, live at peace with everyone." Be the catalyst for peace to everyone, including your family, your friends, your teammates, and even your enemies.

DELIGHT

How did you feel as you read today's Scripture? Were you doubtful? Sarcastic? Wide-eyed? Why did you feel that way?

What does it mean to "live in harmony with one another" (v. 16)? What would it take to do that?

According to verses 19-20, what happens when we choose not to take revenge?

DISPLAY

One of the key words in today's passage is "everyone." As in, "live at peace with everyone." And that literally means everyone. Not just the people you like. Not just the people who are kind. And definitely not just your friends. There are probably even a few people who have come to mind and you thought, "There's no possible way I can live at peace with them!" But I challenge you to take God at His Word and take the first step at living out that transformed mind. Today, go out of your way to be kind and live at peace with one new person.

God so loved the world that He gave Jesus to bring His peace to humanity. As we live out His example, we must remember that this is why we do it: God loved us even when we were His enemies. He still reached out to us. Begin your prayer time today by thanking God for His salvation and overflowing love.

WHO AM I?

READ 1 PETER 2:1-10.

But you are a chosen race, a royal priesthood, a holy nation, a people for his possession, so that you may proclaim the praises of the one who called you out of darkness into his marvelous light. Once you were not a people, but now you are God's people; you had not received mercy, but now you have received mercy.
— *1 Peter 2:9-10*

DISCOVER

When I was in middle school, I loved playing the piano. I had been taking lessons for years, and I loved to practice and perform. For Christmas one year, my uncle gave me some classical piano music, and I couldn't wait to try playing it. But when I took it home and sat down to play, I realized it was way over my head. I couldn't make it through the first page! My uncle saw me not as a middle-school pianist but as a polished musician. He didn't buy that book for me as I was at that time but for me as I would be in ten years. (And I'm happy to report that I played those pieces in college!)

God sees us the same way in today's passage. Peter describes us as "a chosen race, a royal priesthood, a holy nation, a people for his possession, so that you might proclaim the praises [of God]" (v. 9). You may not describe yourself that way, but God wants you to hear this clearly: this is who you really are if you are His child through faith in Jesus.

It can be hard to believe our identity in Christ when we struggle so much. But that's the essence of a transformed mind: we choose to believe God's Word when it tells us who we are, even if we don't feel it. God doesn't require you to be perfect in order to be part of His kingdom. He called you and He will be faithful to help you grow up in your faith. You can believe it!

Read back over Romans 12:3-18. What are the similarities between this and 1 Peter 2:1-2?

How does 1 Peter 2:9 help us understand our identity in Christ?

DISPLAY

If you found out tomorrow that you were a prince or princess of a faraway nation, you'd start acting differently. That's not so different from what we read today. God's description of you is majestic and amazing! So, knowing you are declared chosen, royal, holy, and a living stone, how should you live? As you go through life, it should affect your attitude, words, actions, and plans. You've been called out of darkness into the light of Jesus. Live your moments as the righteous, beloved, holy child whom He has said you are. Let Him give you a new mindset.

As you pray, consider the words of 1 Peter 2:9 and write them down in your prayer journal. Let those key words guide you. Invite God to help you know and believe who He is and who you are, finding your firm foundation in Jesus Christ, the honored cornerstone.

DAY 16

BRAND NEW NAME

READ GENESIS 17:1-14.

*"Your name will no longer be Abram; your name will be Abraham,
for I will make you the father of many nations."*
— Genesis 17:5

DISCOVER

At this point in Scripture, Abram had already had many experiences with God. He had been called from his homeland to go hundreds of miles away. He had settled down in a new land at God's direction. He had faced challenges, and he had fought battles, each time finding God to be faithful even when Abram wasn't.

In today's verses, God appears to Abram and makes a covenant, a binding oath between them. The passage begins with a statement of God's identity (God Almighty), followed by a command ("live in my presence and be blameless") and a promise ("I will multiply you greatly"). This covenant reveals God's intent to always be with Abram. In response to this promise, the man of God "fell facedown" (v. 3).

The next part of the covenant is our focus: God wanted to change Abram's identity, so He changed Abram's name to Abraham. Abraham's old name means "exalted father"; the new name means "father of a multitude." That may seem like an outlandish promise and name change for a man who was ninety-nine years old and had been unable to have children to this point with his wife Sarai, let alone enough children to begin a nation. But God's promise was sure. It would happen.

When God does something new in someone's life in the Bible, He often changes that person's name. Abram became Abraham because God was going to make him the father of many nations. Having a renewed mind means believing God can do what He said He will do!

What specific things did God promise to Abraham? What did He require from Abraham?

How long would God's covenant last, according to verse 7? Why is that important for us?

Who would be the recipients of this promise (v. 8)? How does this affect you?

DISPLAY

Abraham isn't the only person who received promises from God; the Bible is full of promises that still apply to us today! But like Abraham, we must recognize that God is the source of faithfulness and blessing for every promise. So, we live genuinely before Him, seeking to be obedient and humble. Look up Isaiah 41:10, John 16:33, and Psalm 32:8 and either write these verses on some index cards or type them in your phone. As you go through your day, read these verses, and ask God to help you believe His promises and lean on His faithfulness.

Before you pray today, pause and think of a song or hymn that points to the faithfulness of God. (You might consider "Great is Thy Faithfulness" or "Faithfulness of God.") Sing this song before you pray, focusing on God's ability to do all He promised, and let its words shape your prayer.

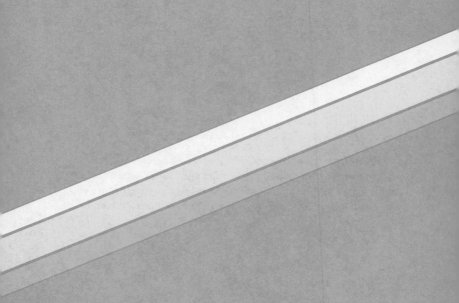

MEMORY VERSE

DO NOT BE CONFORMED
TO THIS AGE, BUT BE
TRANSFORMED BY THE
RENEWING OF YOUR
MIND, SO THAT YOU MAY
DISCERN WHAT IS THE

GOOD, PLEASING, AND PERFECT WILL OF GOD.

ROMANS 12:2

DAY 17

GOD'S PRINCESS

READ GENESIS 17:15-27.

God said to Abraham, "As for your wife Sarai, do not
call her Sarai, for Sarah will be her name."
— Genesis 17:15

DISCOVER

Abraham's new name was a reflection of his new identity in God
(see Gen. 17:1-14). But since God's covenant included a promised family,
Abraham's wife would also need to be included. So Sarai, meaning "my
princess," became Sarah, which simply means "princess." Sarah wouldn't
just be a special woman to one man; she would be a blessing to everyone
who would ever live.

God's new identity for Sarah didn't just stop with her name; it also
included blessings. She would have a son, and her descendants would
include kings. Abraham actually fell down when he heard the news
and laughed with joy at the seemingly impossible promise. But God
specializes in the impossible. Abraham and Sarah's son, Isaac, would
be the father of Jacob, who would be the father of the twelve tribes of
Israel. From one of these tribes would come King David, and ultimately,
King Jesus.

Abraham was ninety-nine when he got his new name; Sarah was ninety.
She had been a childless woman, which in those times was considered
to be a curse. Part of Sarah's challenge was to leave behind her old
childless identity and to embrace the new one. This also caused a change
in Abraham's and Sarah's lives, as the Bible describes in verses 18-26. But
Abraham and Sarah had faith; they believed that God would take care of
the details as they lived obediently in faith.

What did God say twice in verse 16? Why do you think God repeated this part of the promise?

Does laughter seem like an appropriate response to God (v. 17)? Why do you think Abraham laughed at the news God brought him?

DISPLAY

God's promises are often so life-changing that we can hardly believe them. Sarah likely believed her child-bearing days were long gone—until Abraham told her the news of God's promise. Like Abraham and Sarah, sometimes we will struggle to believe God's plan and timing are for the best. But we can practice living in faith by choosing every day to trust His commands, His Word, and His love for us. We will only know God's plan if we're in His Word, so re-commit to or keep on reading, studying, memorizing, and meditating on it today.

As you pray, ask God to reveal clearly that He will bless you. God's promise of a son was going to change Sarah's life, and she needed to hear clearly that it would be a blessing! God's plans for your life might not always seem like blessings, but you can believe that they are.

STRUGGLE AND TRIUMPH

READ GENESIS 32:24-32.

"Your name will no longer be Jacob," he said. "It will be Israel because you have struggled with God and with men and have prevailed."
— Genesis 32:28

DISCOVER

Over the past few days, we've read about how God changed Abram and Sarai's names to Abraham and Sarah and how these name changes reflected their identity changes as well as necessary transformation of their minds. It's an amazing story and a spiritual concept that we should consider deeply.

But what if one person's identity is changed and it affects an entire nation? That's what happened in the life of Jacob. He was the son of Isaac, who was the promised son of Abraham and Sarah. And just like his grandparents, Jacob had his name changed by God. In Genesis 32, Jacob is preparing for the most difficult moment of his life: he's about to come face-to-face with his brother, Esau. A brother with whom he has a complicated, painful history (see Gen. 25).

On the eve of the encounter with Esau, Jacob found himself in a wrestling match with an unknown opponent. Turns out that the unknown opponent was God Himself. And although Jacob would limp for the rest of his life as a reminder of it, he also walked away with a new identity: one who struggled with God. Through it, his name became Israel, which would also be the name of his descendants and the nation they would become. They, too, would struggle with God.

Even in the struggle, Jacob found blessing. Even though he walked away with a limp, Jacob found his identity. Even though struggle would mark his life, Jacob had been transformed inside and out by God Himself.

According to verse 24, how long did Jacob wrestle with the mysterious opponent? Who do you think won the match? Why?

Why do you think Jacob expected a blessing from his foe? Why do you think Jacob asked Him for His name?

DISPLAY

Like Jacob, you may find yourself struggling with God. Perhaps you don't understand why the Bible teaches you to act a certain way. Maybe you're struggling with obedience. Or you might even not understand His timing or plan. That was part of Jacob's story, and it's probably part of yours. But as God's children, we must never let go of Him. We must continue to cling to Him, to His Word, and to His love for us until we fully trust that He is with us and He is faithful. Today, consider how completely you are committed to sticking with the Lord through the good, bad, hard, easy, beautiful, and ugly times. Commit to stick with Him—He's sticking with you forever!

Jacob didn't only struggle with God; he also struggled with other people (see v. 28). You may be struggling with a friend, a family member, or an acquaintance today. As you pray, lay those names and those struggles before the Lord, entrusting the situation to His mighty presence.

DAY 19

WHO AM I?

READ MATTHEW 16:13-20.

*"And I also say to you that you are Peter, and on this rock I will build
my church, and the gates of Hades will not overpower it."*
— Matthew 16:18

DISCOVER

By the time of today's Scripture reading, Jesus had begun His public
ministry and had chosen some disciples. Those disciples had heard His
teaching, had watched Him perform miracles, and had experienced His
power over nature. He had even sent them out to go into different towns
to proclaim that the kingdom of God was near.

Just because these people had heard, seen, and experienced Jesus, that
didn't mean they had been transformed by Him yet. And although Jesus
had lived with these men and poured His life into them, He still wanted
them to articulate the truth of who He is. So when Jesus asked, "Who do
people say that [I am]?" they gave a variety of answers: John the Baptist,
Elijah, Jeremiah, or another of the great prophets. Each of these men had
done amazing things, but none were still living.

Jesus then pointed the question at His disciples: *Who do you, specifically,
say that I am?* Simon Peter, always ready to speak, answered: "You
are the Messiah, the Son of the living God" (v. 16). Boom—correct
answer! And because this Spirit-inspired answer revealed a mind being
transformed by God, Jesus responded by changing Simon's name to
Peter, meaning "rock." Peter's description of Jesus was the solid rock of
faith for all Christians.

Peter's confession indicated that his identity had been changed. Your
identity has been changed as well once your place your faith in Jesus. He
is the rock, the only foundation to trust your life upon.

Why do you think Jesus began this discussion by asking who people thought He was?

Does Jesus really know everything? If so, why do you think He asked these questions?

What does the word "Messiah" mean? Why was it significant then and why is it significant now?

DISPLAY

Many people use this very discussion to start a conversation with unbelievers about Jesus. It's a non-threatening way to begin a spiritual conversation: "Who do you think Jesus is?" As they did two thousand years ago, people today give a variety of answers. Some say, "He was a good man" or "He was a teacher" or maybe even "He was a fraud." But we who know and believe Peter's answer know who He really is. Pray about an opportunity to bring up this conversation with an unbeliever in the coming days. Be ready to share who He is and how He has changed you.

As you pray, read slowly through verses 19-20. Invite God to help you understand the significance of these verses. Your life on earth has an impact on heavenly things. Invite the Lord to guide you as you consider how you are representing the heavenly kingdom as you go through your life today.

THE ABSOLUTE WORST

READ ACTS 9:10-19.

*But the Lord said to him, "Go, for this man is my chosen instrument
to take my name to Gentiles, kings, and Israelites."*
— *Acts 9:15*

DISCOVER

Think of the worst person you know. Perhaps his language is filthy in every situation. Perhaps she is cruel and mean towards everyone. Maybe he even causes harm to himself or others. Whoever it is for you, most of us can identify that one "worst" person.

In the days of the early church, that person was Saul. He had charisma, education, influence, and a killer resume. He proclaimed that zeal for God drove him, but really it was hatred for Christ followers. He did everything in his power to put an end to them. That is, until he came face to face with Jesus Himself. Blind and utterly confused, Saul was led to Damascus.

That's when God called on a believer named Ananias, instructing him to go to Saul and to work a miracle to restore his sight. Ananias responded like we might have responded: "No thanks, Lord. You've heard about this guy, right? He's the worst!" But God knew not only that the change in Saul was genuine but that Saul would be His mouthpiece all over the world. God knew Saul would travel thousands of miles and help bring many people to saving faith in Jesus.

God would eventually change Saul's name to Paul, but the internal change had already occurred. Jesus had entered his life, forgiven him, and called him to a mission to glorify Him alone. This story is evidence of how God can transform the minds, hearts, and the lives of even "the absolute worst" people.

When was a time you witnessed God bringing about a radical transformation in someone's life?

What happened to Saul when Ananias came and placed hands on him? What do you think that represented?

DISPLAY

Most believers fervently pray that God would use us to bring our unbelieving loved ones to saving faith in Jesus, and we look forward to those opportunities. But every so often, God points us toward someone not so loved—a bully, a rebel, a hater, a fighter. Like Ananias, we may initially recoil. But hear God's heart: He loves that person and wants you to receive the blessing of sharing salvation. You might think you're crazy to think a horrible person can change, but it happened with Saul! God's transformation is amazingly powerful. Never write off the power of God's transforming grace.

As you pray, reflect on the things Ananias did to obey God: he went to the place God had instructed, he touched Saul's eyes, and he spoke truth. You can do the same: obey God, go where He sends, touch others, and speak truth. Offer yourself to do these things in God's name today.

A NEW LIFE

You may have a basic life plan in the back of your mind. It probably includes your education, your job, your relationships, and your lifestyle. But Jesus gives us a new life with new blessings, new challenges, and new perspectives. His new, amazing plan probably isn't what you had in mind, but it's perfect for you!

DAY 21

HOLY WEAPON

READ ROMANS 6:1-14.

*And do not offer any parts of it to sin as weapons for unrighteousness.
But as those who are alive from the dead, offer yourselves to God, and
all the parts of yourselves to God as weapons for righteousness.*
— *Romans 6:13*

DISCOVER

We closed out the last section of this book learning about God not only changing Saul's name but also his heart, his mind, his identity, and his mission. Geared up with his new identity and a zeal for Jesus, Saul (who became Paul) spent the rest of his life making Christ known. He went on three missionary journeys, and when he wasn't traveling, he spent time writing letters to the Christians he had led to Jesus.

The book of Romans is one such letter. Paul used this letter to answer the foundational questions that a new follower of Christ might ask. The Christians at that time had heard of grace but had figured that the grace of God nullified anything they did wrong. If grace was so great, why even worry about living obediently?

Paul answered this question boldly and passionately: grace is amazing, but our old sinful selves have been crucified. We don't choose to live for sin and its actions; we choose to live dead to sin so that we can be alive for Christ. Paul had an old self; so did every person who's ever come to saving faith. But that old self is gone, and through salvation we have a new self, a new mind, and a new perspective. Because of that, we choose to flee from sin. Our new life—every single part of it—is offered to God as a weapon for righteousness (see v. 13).

What kind of newness is Paul talking about in verse 4? How does this new life connect to a new mind?

According to verse 11, how should we see our new selves? How does that affect our everyday walk with Jesus?

The debate about willfully living in sin it is still a stumbling block for Christians today. But Paul's words, so powerful two thousand years ago, still hold true today: we are new creations, with new minds, and new lives. Because of that, we choose to be used by God as weapons of righteousness—thinking righteously, living righteously, and revealing righteousness. Righteousness is an outward reflection of an inward devotion to our holy God. Is your life marked by righteousness? Or are you falling for the lie that God's grace means it's okay to keep sinning?

As you pray today, consider carefully the words of today's key verse. Prayerfully think through the different parts of your body: mind, hands, mouth, arms, feet, even knees. How might you offer each of these to the Lord as weapons or instruments of righteousness?

SINGING GOD'S SONG

READ PSALM 40.

*He put a new song in my mouth, a hymn of praise to our God.
Many will see and fear, and they will trust in the LORD.*
— Psalm 40:3

DISCOVER

David lived his life openly before the Lord. He was always willing to pray and sing about his struggles, his joys, his fears, and his enemies. If you ever want to see the highs and lows of a person who is doing his best to seek the Lord, go to the psalms of David.

In Psalm 40, we don't know the exact situation David was in, but we know it was a trial. He had been crying out to the Lord for help (v. 1). God heard him and brought him up out of the muddy pit of his situation, making his steps secure (v. 2). It probably doesn't surprise you that singer/songwriter David burst into song following God's salvation.

Did you catch where the song came from? David said, "*He* put a new song in my mouth, a hymn of praise to our God" (v. 3, emphasis added). The deliverance came from God, and so did the song. That's what God does in the life of someone who has trusted Him to be the ultimate Savior and Lord.

David, king of Israel, realized the great impact this story would have on his friends and citizens: "Many will see and fear, and they will trust in the Lord" (v. 3). It doesn't just happen when kings recognize God's deliverance; anyone who has been changed by God's saving grace has a new song to sing. David points to a life of faith in these verses: waiting patiently, crying out, and singing praise when salvation comes. These are marks of a new life!

What kind of situation comes to your mind when you hear the descriptors "desolate pit" or "muddy clay?" How has God saved you from situations like this in the past?

What song has been in your heart today? When was the last time you sang a song of praise someplace other than in a church?

DISPLAY

Many Christians don't know how to share their faith or give their testimony—it seems too overwhelming. But David gives a great example of a testimony in the first three verses of this psalm: he describes his situation before God, he points to how God heard his cry, he explains how God changed his situation, and he praises God for all he has done. This sequence can be summarized simply: "Before God . . . then God . . . and now God . . ." Consider how you might give a similar testimony to a friend or family member. Write it out in the space below:

Before God

Then God

Now God

As you pray today, consider the rest of the words found in Psalm 40. Pray the psalm aloud, slowly and deliberately, carefully considering the words. Are any of David's statements true of you? Do you delight to do God's will (v. 8)? Do you consider His instructions (v. 8)? Do you speak of God openly (vv. 9-10)? Ask God to give you the desire to do these things.

DAY 23

PUTTING AWAY

READ EPHESIANS 4:17-32.

*And be kind and compassionate to one another, forgiving
one another, just as God also forgave you in Christ.*
— *Ephesians 4:32*

DISCOVER

How often do you put things away? You probably put books away in your locker at the end of the day. You probably help around the house by putting away laundry or dishes. Your grandmother might even joke that you can "put away some food."

In today's verses, Paul is writing to his friends to help them live genuine Christian lives. He contrasts those who know God with those who don't, revealing that sin marks the lives of people who don't have a heart for God. He then instructs them to remove their former (sinful) lives and "to be renewed in the spirit of [their] minds" (v. 23), putting on their new selves.

Putting on the new self requires putting away some other things, such as lying, anger, dishonesty, foul language, bitterness, wrath, shouting, slander, and malice (vv. 25-31). A new self simply cannot walk around in these "old self" characteristics! Instead, we speak truth, work honestly, share, and speak words that build up.

The instructions in verse 32 complete the statement: be kind, compassionate, and forgiving. Why? Because God forgave us. The new self is created according to who God is (v. 24), so our new lives reflect Him. We can imagine that the Christians in Ephesus may have gotten a little overwhelmed at Paul's words; these counter-cultural characteristics were just as difficult to live out then as they are today. But that's the point: we don't live like everyone else after we come to know Christ. We live according to a new life!

Write out everything Paul instructs believers to "put away" in these verses. Which one of these do you need the most help putting away in your life?

Now write out everything we're supposed to do or embrace. Circle one element that you could be more intentional in acting on and write out a way you can move on this realization.

In these verses, Paul points out several things we should and shouldn't do. Each of the items on the list will be difficult for one person but easy for the next. Perhaps you struggle with anger but have no problem speaking honestly. Don't let your strengths and weaknesses get you down! Instead, praise God for helping you live righteously in some areas and ask Him to help you live righteously in the areas where you struggle. God loves to hear us admit we need His help (see 2 Cor. 12:9), and He will help us!

As you pray, begin by thanking God for all He has done for you. He's shown you mercy, grace, forgiveness, compassion, kindness, and love. Then read slowly through today's passage, considering how you can better reflect your heavenly Father in living out these words from Paul!

DAY 24

LOVE AND DIRTY FEET

READ JOHN 13:1-20,34-45.

"I give you a new command: Love one another. Just as I have loved you, you are also to love one another. By this everyone will know that you are my disciples, if you love one another."
— John 13:34-35

DISCOVER

I had a job in an office building when I was in high school. One day, I noticed one of the ceiling tiles in a hallway was moved, and a big bucket was under it, catching water dripping down. I was shocked to see the owner of the company, not a maintenance worker, soaking up the water with towels.

A good leader never asks someone to do something he wouldn't do himself. You won't be surprised to hear that this is exactly how Jesus led: by example. John introduces today's reading by explaining that the last days of Jesus's life were upon Him. He loved His disciples and He wanted them to see clearly His desire that they love one another. So, before the Passover feast, He washed all their feet. That "all" included Judas, who had already made plans to betray Jesus.

The disciples didn't really understand what Jesus was doing, and that was okay; they would understand it all after He had died and risen again. We can only imagine their thoughts: "Jesus, do you realize how dirty our feet are? Have you ever seen Matthew's feet? We can wash our own feet!" But Jesus was living out the calling He gives to His followers: love.

Jesus's definition of love isn't like the world's. He calls us to love both those who love us back and those who would harm us. This includes the hypocrite, the bully, and the disgruntled. But when we love like Jesus loved, everyone will know we belong to Him. This is new life!

DELIGHT

Read verses 1-3 carefully. What did Jesus know? How did this knowledge lead Him as He washed His disciples' feet?

What was Simon Peter's response to having his feet washed? Why do you think he said that?

Jesus demonstrated that washing of feet—a dirty, menial task—reveals love. This was the way Jesus chose to demonstrate love in that setting, but of course, it's not the only way. Any sacrificial act of loving others reveals that the love of Jesus is in us. Loving like this may involve playing a silly game with your little sister, helping your grandmother work a puzzle, being kind to the weird kid in your class, or smiling at that grumpy guy at the grocery story. Today, make a plan for how you can show love to people every time you enter a building.

As you pray today, slowly read John 13:34-35, focusing on the word "command." Jesus didn't suggest that we love—He commanded it. Offer the depths of your heart to the Lord. How well do you love? Where your heart is hard, confess that and invite Christ's love to fill you.

THE LIGHT OF LOVE

READ 1 JOHN 2:3-11.

*The one who says he is in the light but hates his
brother or sister is in the darkness until now.*
— 1 John 2:9

DISCOVER

Yesterday you saw Jesus demonstrate His love by washing the feet of His disciples. That passage was recorded by John, a disciple of Jesus and the author of the Gospel named after him. Today's passage is written by that same disciple, only this book is a letter, or epistle, he wrote to believers.

We know that Jesus washed John's feet, and obviously the lesson stuck with the disciple, because love was the theme of this letter he wrote. He helps us understand love by linking it to obedience (see 1 John 2:3). Basically, he explains it like this: if we know Jesus, we keep His commands; that includes the commands to love God and love others. So love is the proof—to us as well as to others—that we belong to Jesus (vv. 3-6).

John's words aren't ambiguous or lofty. He doesn't teach that we should pretend like we love. Instead, he specifically points out that people who don't love one another don't truly love God. Love comes from God, flows through us, and is evident to the people around us. We don't always want to love, and some people are really difficult to love. But that doesn't excuse us from it. If you've been given a new life in Jesus, love should mark each of your relationships.

There is no room for hatred in the heart of a believer, for we have been saved by the One who loved the world enough to give His one and only Son (see John 3:16).

What self-check does John give in verse 4? How would John assess your love for others?

What do you think "light" and "darkness" mean in these verses? What is John revealing?

DISPLAY

In Matthew 5, Jesus instructs us to "let your light shine before others, so that they may see your good works and give glory to your Father in heaven" (v. 16). This reflects the point that John is making in today's verses: we are a visible light to a dark world when we live for Jesus. Sometimes we want to avoid the attention others may give us, but Jesus (and John) affirm that living in love will be seen because it is light. Commit to being a light in your home, school, and world today, knowing that your light—God's light—will shine when you love others.

Before you pray, read 1 John 2:9 aloud twice, and then try to quote it without looking. Then, quietly meditate on the verse as you invite the Lord to let you see how seriously you take these words. Do you hate, or do you love? The answer reveals your heart.

DAY 26

NEW, OLD LOVE

READ 2 JOHN 1-13.

This is love: that we walk according to his commands. This is the command as you have heard it from the beginning: that you walk in love.
— 2 John 6

DISCOVER

In John's Gospel, the author never identified himself by name. Instead, he called himself "the one Jesus loved" (see John 13:23; 20:2; 21:7; 21:20). Obviously, John found his identity in the love of Jesus.

Though John was changed by the love of Jesus, it wasn't a new thought. In Exodus, God passed in front of Moses and gives this declaration: "The LORD—the LORD is a compassionate and gracious God, slow to anger and abounding in faithful love and truth, maintaining faithful love to a thousand generations, forgiving iniquity, rebellion, and sin" (Ex. 34:6-7). God was the embodiment of love, as is Jesus, who was fully God in a human body.

As John addresses love in this second epistle, he takes a minute to point out that love isn't a new command, but something that God taught from the beginning. God is love, so His children are to reflect that in our lives. What is new, then, is us. The life we have in Jesus makes us long to love others with genuine, God-glorifying love.

Just like in yesterday's verses, we see John tie love to living in obedience. Love means walking according to God's commands (see v. 6). That might seem to be a stretch, but remember who God is: the I AM. So if we truly believe He is who He says He is, we obey Him.

Who do you think John is referring to as the "elect lady" (v. 1) and the "dear lady" (v. 5)? Why wouldn't John just use their names?

According to verses 7-11, how should we react to people who try to deceive us in God's teachings?

DISPLAY

Consider the word "walk": it's how most of us travel, get from place to place, and move around. Some people walk fast, some walk slowly, and some walk with style. John's words in today's passage point to our spiritual walk. Are you loving as you go through your day? Is obedience marking the style of your walk? Your everyday life reveals your walk of faith. Is your everyday life revealing love and obedience? If it isn't, it's time to confess that and ask Jesus to teach you to walk in the newness of the life He has given you.

As you pray, consider carefully John's words in verse 12. He didn't want to use any more paper and ink; he wanted to see his fellow Christians face to face "so that [their] joy may be complete" (v. 12). Thank God for the Christians in your life who bring you joy!

MEMORY VERSE

THEN THE ONE
SEATED ON THE
THRONE SAID,

"**LOOK,**
I AM MAKING
EVERYTHING

NEW."
HE ALSO SAID,
"WRITE, BECAUSE
THESE WORDS
ARE FAITHFUL
AND TRUE."

REVELATION 21:5

NEW COVENANT, NEW LIFE

READ LUKE 22:14-23.

In the same way he also took the cup after supper and said, "This cup is the new covenant in my blood, which is poured out for you."
— Luke 22:20

DISCOVER

God's Word is marked with covenants—solemn promises between God and His people. He had a covenant with Noah not to destroy the earth again with a flood. He made a covenant with Abraham to be with him and bless him in the new land. He made a covenant with David to keep a descendant of his on the throne of Israel.

God was faithful to keep His covenants, and Jesus brought a new covenant through His life and death. The covenant of Jesus didn't undo the old covenants; on the contrary, He fulfilled the old covenant through His sacrifice on the cross. In today's Scripture, Jesus is giving His disciples a little insight into the new covenant. In the midst of His last meal with His closest friends, He helped them understand this new covenant.

For centuries before Jesus, God's people had brought their animal sacrifices to the temple as offerings to the Lord for their sin; when Jesus died, He fulfilled that old-covenant requirement. If you haven't noticed, we're not bringing our calves and goats to slaughter at an altar any more! Instead, we have a new covenant, found only in the blood of Jesus, which He poured out for us. This amazingly merciful and loving sacrifice by Jesus is the reason we can live new, transformed lives. Jesus knew His sacrificial death would bring life to all who would find new life in Him.

Read verses 14-18 carefully. What was Jesus trying to explain? Then read verse 23. Do you think the disciples understood His message that night?

According to verse 19, what did the bread represent? How was that fulfilled on the cross?

DISPLAY

If these words sound familiar to you, that means you've participated in your church's observance of the Lord's Supper. As Jesus and His disciples took the bread and the cup, He instructed them to "do this in remembrance of me" (v. 19). We repeat these same words each time we observe the Lord's Supper in our churches. Take time to prepare yourself spiritually for this holy observance. Prayerfully remember Christ's sacrifice, thank Him for salvation through His blood, confess your sins, and commit your new life in Christ to His glory. Remember that this observance is part of your testimony.

As you pray, re-read verses 14-18 and consider Jesus's emotions. He "fervently desired" (v. 14) to eat the Passover, He gave thanks (v. 17), and He instructed His disciples to share the cup (v. 17). Spend some time meditating on Jesus's great sacrifice on the cross and His great joy in making it available to His followers.

DAY 28

NEW EVERY MORNING

READ LAMENTATIONS 3:19-33.

Because of the LORD's faithful love we do not perish, for his mercies never end. They are new every morning; great is your faithfulness! I say, "The LORD is my portion, therefore I will put my hope in him."
— Lamentations 3:22-24

DISCOVER

Jeremiah, who many believe wrote the book of Lamentations, was a prophet who lived during a time of great turmoil. God's people had rejected Him for many years, and He was allowing their enemies, the Babylonians, to triumph over Israel. It was a horrible, terrible time for Jeremiah and all the Israelites living at that time. The Babylonians were ruthless, and many people who weren't killed by the sword died of starvation and disease.

Jeremiah had warned the Israelites about their idolatry and apathy; they had not listened. He had prayed for them, preached to them, and done everything to demonstrate what God demanded; nobody changed their hearts. In the book of Lamentations, we see how this horrible situation gripped him.

But even as he watched his friends and neighbors die and experienced the horror of siege and attack, Jeremiah chose to remember God's faithfulness. He was depressed (v. 20), so he chose to remember God in the midst of his terror. And what did he remember? God has faithful love and mercy that is new every morning (v. 22-23).

New every single morning! No matter how bad your yesterday was or how afraid you are for tomorrow, God will pour out new faithful love and mercy. Jeremiah's words came at one of the darkest periods of Israel's history. If God's mercy and love were new in that time, they are new for us, as well! As we wait for God's salvation (vv. 25-26), we put our hope in Him (v. 24).

99

MADE NEW

In your Bible, underline every description of God that you find in today's verses. What do these things teach you about God?

According to verses 25-30, what are some good things for God's people to do? How well do you do these things?

DISPLAY

All of us have good days and bad days. But God's faithful love and mercy are with all of His people on every single day, even if it's our own sin that brings about our situation. It's tough to believe God's Word and hope in Him when we're struggling, hurting, or overwhelmed. So in those times, we must do as Jeremiah did: choose to remember who God is and what He has done. In your prayer journal, start writing down verses that remind you to believe God and hope in Him.

Jeremiah didn't sugarcoat his situation. These verses explain that he was afflicted, homeless, and depressed (vv. 19-20). So as you pray today, don't pretend that everything is okay if it's not; pour out your heart and invite God to step into your life and your struggles. Don't forget to choose to hope before you leave your time of prayer!

DAY 29

SLAVE TO SOMETHING

READ ROMANS 6:15-23.

*What then? Should we sin because we are not under
the law but under grace? Absolutely not!*
— Romans 6:15

DISCOVER

Slavery is a sad part of human history. Throughout most of history, groups of people have taken control over other groups of people. It's a terrible thing: rights are removed, dignity is ignored, and power over another human being is viewed as the reward for the mighty.

Though slavery is illegal in most parts of the world today, the practice is unfortunately still alive and well in many ways. There is also a different form of slavery that still holds power: each of us is a slave to either sin or righteousness. Either sin will dictate your thoughts, attitudes, hearts, and actions or God's righteousness will. This is the kind of slavery Paul is talking about.

Paul's words to us today point out that some people think they can choose both: they think they can still sin because grace triumphs over it. But Paul reveals the truth behind that false thinking—you can't be righteous and still sin! God commands that His people live righteously according to His definition. We are lying to ourselves and ignoring God's Word when we think we can sin willfully and still call Jesus "Lord."

We're fooling ourselves if we think we aren't slaves to anything. If you aren't choosing to devote yourself to righteousness, you've given control to sin. The question, then, is this: Are you a slave to sin or a slave to God's righteousness? Either one will control your life.

For what reason did Paul instruct his friends to thank God in verses 17-18? Why is this important?

Paul asks a very poignant question in verse 21: What was some fruit being produced in your life before Jesus that you are now ashamed of? Answer this question below.

DISPLAY

Today's passage is a great journaling prompt. After reading
Romans 6:15-23, fill out the chart below. Take a few thoughtful minutes
to jot down what each type of slavery would look like in a situation. In
fact, consider some situations you encountered yesterday and write
which type of slavery you revealed in your actions. Carefully consider your
thankfulness and gratitude to God as you go through today!

Slave to Sin	Slave to Righteousness

Before you pray, meditate on the words of Romans 6:23. You've
probably heard them before, but did they really seep into your
belief system? You once lived in sin, which leads to death. But
God's gift of Jesus leads to eternal life! Praise and thank Him for
that as you pray.

EVERYTHING NEW!

READ REVELATION 21:1-8.

Then the one seated on the throne said, "Look, I am making everything new." He also said, "Write, because these words are faithful and true."
— Revelation 21:5

DISCOVER

For the past twenty-nine days, we've looked at all types of Bible passages that point to being made new. We've considered new names, new identities, new thought patterns, new lives, new paths, and becoming new creatures. We've considered how God renews us as we trust Him.

But the last book of the Bible gives us a truth that is perhaps even more amazing: at the end of time as we know it, God will make everything new. "Everything" meaning everything. Not just me and you, but heaven and earth, as well! There will be a new ocean and a new Jerusalem, and it will come out fresh and new and free of all the sin of the first world.

As amazing as our world and universe is, the new one will be even better because God Himself will live with us. No longer will we be separated from Him; we will have the joy and delight of living with God forever. The things of the old world—tears, death, grief, destruction, and pain—will be gone, as well.

If that all sounds a little far-fetched, I challenge you to consider the One who spoke the words of today's key verse: Jesus Christ, "the Alpha and Omega, the beginning and the end" (v. 6). The One through whom the first world was made (see Col. 1:16) and who made you new most certainly has the power to bring about a new heaven and new earth. His words are faithful and true; don't be afraid to sing for joy at this promise!

DELIGHT

How is the new holy city described in verse 2? What do you think is the significance of this imagery?

What word is repeated in verse 3 and verse 5? Why do you think that word is there? What does it remind us to do?

DISPLAY

Christians are dramatically different from everyone else on earth because of our belief about eternity: God is eternal, and His people will live eternally with Him. That's not just good news for eternity—it's good news for today! That truth should change your outlook, your hope, your attitude, and the way you approach problems. We can approach death, grief, tears, and pain with hope and joy because we know they won't last. Dwell on these verses at each struggle today; focusing on eternity will change your moments right now.

Before you pray, re-read today's verses and try to imagine what they describe in your mind's eye. See the old heaven and earth pass away, and watch the new Jerusalem come down out of heaven. Imagine looking God in the eye. Now offer your prayers, knowing that this promise is reality.

SPIRITUAL DISCIPLINE MASHUP

When you hear the words "spiritual discipline" you probably hone in on the word "discipline." Maybe your mind starts spinning and you think it sounds formal, scholarly, or even boring. Let's set straight what this phrase really means, then we'll mix it up a bit and show you some fun ways to strengthen your faith. "Spiritual disciplines" is simply a term for different methods you can use to grow closer to God. They can fit into three categories: **inward**, **outward**, and **corporate** (which in this case means "shared by a group," like with the word "incorporated").[1] A few examples of these are:

> **Inward Disciplines** — Bible study, prayer, meditation, and fasting

> **Outward Discipline** — Service, solitude, submission, and simplicity

> **Corporate Disciplines** — Worship, celebration, confession, and guidance

That's a lot, right? For today, we'll just focus on the first four—the inward disciplines. Here's a quick overview:

> **Bible Study** — This is more than just reading a passage of Scripture; this is a deep dive into context, theological meaning, and personal application. For our exercises here, choose a book of the Bible and focus on just a few verses at a time.

> **Prayer** — Prayer is a conversation with God, but it's important to focus on listening and hearing from God. Remember that it's not about getting what you want from God—it's about connecting with Him.

> **Meditation** — The point of meditating is to slow down and focus your mind and heart on God. You can do this by considering who He is and what He has done or by dwelling on a specific Scripture verse.

Fasting — Essentially, fasting is giving something up and using the time you would have spent on that thing to focus on God instead. The most common way to fast is to give up food for a time, but you can also fast from things like TV, social media, screen time, video games, and so on. Be aware of your personal needs and health, but try to choose the thing that consumes most of your time and attention.

Now, let's look at some fun ways to try out these spiritual disciplines. Grab a six-sided die, a jar, and several slips of paper.

Start by writing out each of the following ideas on individual slips of paper or index cards. Fold the slips of paper and put them in the jar.

BIBLE STUDY

- Read the passage in multiple Bible translations.

- Use a Bible dictionary or search the internet and look up words that stand out to you.

- Make a thirty-second video explaining what you just read.

- Mark up the passage with different colored highlighters to represent things like theme, audience, writer, or words that repeat.

- Write a one- to two-sentence summary of what you read.

- Look up a list of attributes of God. Note which ones you see in the passage and how.

- Find passages with similar themes or connected timelines and read those.

- Allow a Bible app to read the passage aloud to you.

- Try Bible journaling.

- Create a symbol key and use it to note common words or themes as you study a specific book.

- Meet with a friend, family member, or faith mentor for thirty minutes in person or over the phone to discuss what you've been reading.

PRAYER

- Keep a prayer journal.

- Try one of the prayer models like **ACTS**, **PRAY**, **HEAR**, or **SOAP**. Look them up online if you don't know what these prayer models are.

- Pray a specific verse that you love or that stood out to you from this devotional.

- Say a prayer aloud.

- Go for a walk and pray over the people in that area or what God might have you do there.

- Pray with a friend, family member, or faith mentor.

MEDITATION

- Write out each word of a key verse on index cards. Mix the cards up, then reorder them, reading aloud when you do.

- Set a timer for five minutes and sit quietly, focusing on who God is.

- Look up a list of the attributes of God on the internet. Choose one and consider how God displays that attribute in your life.

- Be curious. Consider what's going on in your life, what might be distracting you from God, and how God is working in your heart.

- Focus on a specific passage of Scripture in the Gospels, imagining it as if you were there. Consider how you would feel, what you would see, smell, taste, or hear, and so on.

FASTING

- During the time when you'd normally eat lunch, spend time in prayer or serving someone nearby.

- Remove your social media apps from your phone and don't log in online for a set amount of time, like a month, a week, or even just a day. Notice how many times you reach for your phone. Each time you want to reach for your phone, reach out to God instead.

- Instead of watching a TV show, pick up your Bible or a book that teaches you something new about God. Read for the same duration as the show.

- If you play video games or spend a lot of time scrolling online, try setting aside that time to spend time with family or friends and encourage each other in your faith walk.

- Think of something else you spend a lot of time doing. How could you give it up for a season to focus on God in some way?

WHAT TO DO?

When you're ready to practice one of these things, roll the die to determine where you'll do so. (If the number you rolled doesn't work for you, that's okay! Roll again or just choose the number you prefer.)

1. In your room

2. In your house (you pick the location)

3. Outside (wherever it's safe!)

4. At a coffee shop

5. At a park

6. Your pick!

Once you have your location, draw a slip of paper from the jar to see what spiritual discipline you'll be focusing on. Try to stick with it for at least a week and see how it goes. If you find you're not connecting with God that way, start the process over and try again. The point isn't to do these things in specific ways each time, but figuring out how to connect with God in new ways that work for you.

1. Christina Zimmerman, "What Are Spiritual Disciplines?" Lifeway Voices, July 21, 2021, https://voices. lifeway.com/discipleship-evangelism/what-are-spiritual-disciplines/.

Engage with God's Word.

lifeway.com/teendevotionals

☐ SEARCH AND KNOW

☐ TAKE UP AND FOLLOW

☐ THE SHEPHERD KING

☐ CHARACTER & COURAGE

☐ WORDS OF WISDOM

☐ PIONEER & PERFECTOR

☐ WITH YOU

☐ ROMANS

☐ LOVE AND JUSTICE

☐ CALLED TO THIS

☐ GROWING IN GRATITUDE

☐ GOD WITH US